MW01008789

A.I. - 101

A Primer on Using

Artificial Intelligence in Education

Ryan M. Cameron

Table of Contents

Acknowledgments

I am grateful for the support of the people who helped make this book possible. Additionally, I would like to thank all of the organizations and companies that are featured in this book. You are all trailblazers, creating a new and improved era for education.

I never thought I would write a book, let alone a book on artificial intelligence. I am just a simple teacher with a passion for technology. The tremendous opportunities technology has made available to us all, such as self-publishing has been a game changer in my life and no doubt in the lives of many others. This, my first book is dedicated to all the people who gave me a chance and never doubted I could do great things. Perhaps in an even greater sense, this book is also dedicated to the people who underestimated the path my life would take. I offer this advice to you the reader, don't let a fear of the future prevent you from success in any new endeavor. I hope this text brings some value to your work. Thank you for reading my book!

Introduction

Most of us have heard the warnings. Artificial intelligence or "AI" is here and is expected to rapidly impact the ways in which we live and work. Every industry and organization ranging from healthcare, entertainment, business and of course, education seems to be talking about AI. It is time we invested a few moments into preparing, understanding and responding to the impact AI will have on education. The topic of AI can certainly conjure up lots of intimidating thoughts that involve killer robots, and how they could replace jobs or even control humanity, but that view is primarily due to science fiction. The reality of artificial intelligence is that it can be used on the premise of improving lives and while the use of robots has indeed replaced some jobs, that could not be further from the truth in the world of education.

If you are optimistic about the future of AI, you should be eager to learn about how AI may compliment your teaching, research, and scholarship activities. If you have more concerns than hopes for AI, you might be worried a robot may replace you in the near future. In either scenario, there is no better time than the present to become more familiar with AI and its potential impact. Leadership in education is needed to chart a course for AI so its function will be to positively impact learning outcomes. Education is built upon personal interactions and making provisions for social settings. So, while the education system is experiencing more use of technology than ever before, properly harnessed, AIs purpose could be to assist educators, not replace them. The future for AI in education is not up to the robots to decide, it is up to us!

Here we will discuss the various ways that AI is changing teaching and learning. If you are new to the realm of AI and if you are seeking a practical primer for what AI means for education, this book may be of value to you.

What Is Artificial Intelligence?

Artificial Intelligence is defined as "the creation of intelligent machines that work and react like humans." The research contained in artificial intelligence involves the programming of attributes that replicate the human ability to include problem-solving, accumulation of knowledge, perception, and planning. The feasibility of incorporating common sense and reasoning skills into machines is quite difficult and requires immense supervision to ensure proper classification and analysis.

Bottom line, in order for artificial intelligence to be possible, it must have access to necessary information in order to get the correct answer. This is true in regard to a mathematical equation, answers to geographical questions or the solving of any problem. Furthermore, the access to the information is provided by humans.

While we may hear about artificial intelligence more frequently in the news, it is not brand new. Fewer than ten years following World War II, in 1950 mathematician Alan Turing, posed the question: "Can machines think?" Thus, began the quest of determining if machines had the ability to imitate human intelligence.

In today's world, artificial intelligence is already a part of our daily lives. From vehicles that offer the self-driving and lane assist features to the convenience of receiving feedback from inquiries made to Siri or Alexa for obtaining details regarding the current weather forecast, or providing information for nearby restaurants, shopping or hotels, and then of course there is the use of GPS navigation systems that most everyone has become acclimated to. All of these platforms incorporate artificial intelligence and most of us enjoy the conveniences offered through its use.

In regard to artificial intelligence, there are two primary categories, which are weak AI or strong AI. An example of weak AI would be Siri or Alexa, or virtual personal assistants as a whole. Weak AI is also inclusive of computer programs that incorporate reasoning skills into online games played against a computer or the current capacity of self-driving automobiles. This form of AI is programmed to tackle specific tasks that fall within designated categories and is the replication of human intelligence in the form of reasoning and correction.

As far as the strong AI applications, also referred to as AGI, or artificial general intelligence is comprised of the ability of an artificial intelligence platform to find a solution to something unfamiliar. In order for this to work, there must first be a vast amount of knowledge compiled into one location in order for the computer to derive at the proper response, through analysis of the data available. This form of AI is much more involved and while fascinating, it is the AGI that is perhaps the most feared among the two categories. Why? When you compare the processability of an AI platform to that of a human, the AI system would excel every time with its ability to access the necessary information within a matter of seconds in order to provide an accurate answer.

With that taken into consideration, there is no surprise that the concept of human jobs being replaced with computers or robots would naturally cause apprehension. Not to mention that famous theoretical physicist, Stephen Hawking warned against the possibility that "strong AI would take off on its own, and re-design itself..." However, that fear may be unprecedented because experts highly doubt the possibility of it progressing to that level.

How We Already Use AI

Change is a natural part of life and is for the most part inevitable. Yet, it is feared and rejected by many because of the unfamiliarity associated with it. For years people in the workforce have posed the question as to whether or not they would be replaced by a computer. This is no different in the field of education according to a recent poll conducted by Gallup and Northeastern University.

However, AI already exists in several facets of life, personally, professionally and also in the world of education. Many of us use Siri on Apple devices, or we ask Alexa and Google to relay information for us on the smart devices throughout our homes. On college campuses, artificial intelligence streamlines the admissions process and provides personalized feedback to students on college campuses.

Artificial Intelligence Provides Daily Conveniences
Do you ask your Google device to "start your day" and listen to a rundown of your schedule as you get ready for work? Do you send a verbal request to Alexa for ordering an item while you're in the middle of preparing dinner? Have you recently scheduled an Uber or Lyft? All of these modern-day conveniences are powered by artificial intelligence and most of us have grown quite accustomed to the conveniences.

Fraud Is Monitored with It
Financial companies now have the ability to monitor potentially fraudulent activity through artificial intelligence. When you consider for a moment the world population and the number of credit cards in circulation, it is unfathomable to account for the man-hours that would be required to successfully monitor everything. Also, by the time criminal activity was detected on a stolen credit card, the person could have easily maxed out the card and taken money from your account.

However, through the use of algorithms and AI, systems can detect unusual spending patterns and alert you to the suspicious activity and even freeze accounts for your protection. While many of us have probably experienced the hassle of our accounts being frozen in error thanks to these algorithms, had it been due to fraud, there is no doubt gratitude would have replaced that frustration of inconvenience.

The Autopilot in the Airplane

The term autopilot is normal and when we hear it, not much focus is devoted to it, but if you've ever been on an airplane, it was the autopilot that did much of the flying. In fact, the human pilot of a Boeing 777 spends a short seven minutes actually flying the plane. With a combination of GPS and motion sensors, the autopilot does most of the work, with the actual pilot primarily being responsible for takeoff and landing.

Self-Driving Vehicles

The thought of automobiles having the ability to drive themselves can be alarming to a degree, but the same concept of autopiloting is put into play. While driving an automobile presents many more challenges because of the population typically present on the road, the technology is in existence and being improved in a way that the self-driving vehicles will be better able to predict actions of other drivers. In fact, this technology is at the forefront of being added to semi-trucks as a way of covering more miles and overcoming the drive-time restrictions placed on truck drivers.

GPS Rerouting

Navigation systems are equipped to notify you of traffic congestion or road construction and even suggest alternative routes.

For the most part, we welcome and appreciate these conveniences and added protections that have become a part of everyday life. So, when it is so prevalent in daily life, it makes sense that the educational system should also jump on the bandwagon and take every possible opportunity to improve the ways of learning, teaching and preparing for the real world of careers and adult life. Having access to more tools makes it possible to develop lesson plans that benefit students regardless of their capabilities or learning levels.

AI Companies Powering Education

While companies like Amazon, Apple and Microsoft are already providing resources that make AI a part of everyday life, there are also many companies that focus on bringing AI to the classroom. Here's a look at the work of a few already making a difference in schools.

Brainly
This technology is based on social networking for students and educators and is used in grade school through college. Brainly is based in New York City and there is also an office in Krakow, Poland, where Brainly was first created.

How Brainly Began
Brainly was first launched in 2009 by a group of friends, Michal Borkowski, Lukasz Haluch, and Tomasz Kraus whom all lived in Poland. Michal, co-founder, and CEO of Brainly grew up in Poland. The classes in his school were always small but they enjoyed a collaborative environment where students always helped one another work through lessons. Michal saw many benefits in that learning environment and realized that if 20 kids learn better that way, why not take it to the world. And so Brainly was created in a social community environment where students around the world are able to present questions as well as provide answers to one another.

Students Helping Students Around the World Through Brainly
Brainly helps students prepare for an array of subjects from mathematics, history, physics, Advanced Placement, computer science as well as offering assistance in learning multiple languages. The program not only answers student questions directly with its algorithm design but also provides a collaborative environment for students where they can discuss questions and solve problems on their own. It is used in more than thirty-five countries by millions of students each month and is the largest existing social learning community.

The team at Brainly is dedicated to expanding the learning options for kids of all ages, collaborating with teachers and scholars as well as students and experts like Rutgers University Professor Chirag Shah. Professor Shah shares his talents in developing new advancements for artificial intelligence and machine learning. Shah uses the questions posed by students within the platform to expand Brainly and make it more accommodating for students.

Brainly is considered a human learning platform and as stated by Professor Shah, "All of the content is produced by real people according to their human interests and needs...But behind the scenes machines are helping make the right connections possible."

Content Technologies, Inc.
A development company that incorporates the information from standard classroom textbooks and curriculums into a system where the data is compiled and analyzed so customized learning materials can be developed.

Creator of CTI
Dr. Scott R. Parfitt formed CTI in Notre Dame in the early 1980s. His Ph.D. is in psychology, he has a bachelor's degree in philosophy and he also taught himself various programming languages and shared his knowledge as an instructor at Indiana University, where he taught programming.

Early in his career, Dr. Parfitt created his own software company called Soft Productions and worked with various companies worldwide in the development of technologies that would enhance learning as well as efficiency and profitability. With his love and talents focused on the technological aspects, he created CTI.

Mission of CTI
The mission of CTI is to develop AI applications that will assist people and speed up certain processes in order to free up valuable time. "We believe that time is your most valuable asset."

CTI works with all types of businesses and they have a specific academic unit known as Palitt, which is where the online applications Cram101 and JustTheFacts101 were created.

JustTheFacts101 is similar to the traditional "Cliff Notes" that were popular decades ago and is designed to provide book summaries to students, focusing on condensing down to the most important chapters and save students time from reading entire novels, etc. Additionally, they offer the AI application, Cram101 that is capable of creating practice tests and study guides for students in preparation of exams.

Ivy.AI
Ivy.ai has created a unique application, sparking a new era for highly sophisticated chatbots. Using these chatbots, Ivy.ai offers educational organizations a pathway to answer a gamut of questions day and night. The technology uses AI automation and rules-based machine learning to help schools be more responsive and productive. Ivy.ai chatbots can be placed on a webpage, or within an app. The software learns the most popular and critical questions asked by students and provides the answers, saving time and decreasing student frustrations. Ivy.ai can also be used to aggregate forms, manuals, guidelines, calendars, websites and campus resources, so answers can be retrieved and delivered on-demand, using a customizable chatbot interface. The Ivy.ai bots provide students with 24/7 access to accurate content at their convenience.

Third Space Learning
Developed to address math intervention for elementary schools, Third Space Learning provides tutoring to kid's preparation for standardized exams such as the SAT. Third Space Learning was first launched in 2017 with their first run involving 6000 students throughout 500 different schools and more than 400 math tutors.

Valuable 1-to-1 Tutoring

Third Space Learning provides math tutoring that addresses specific challenges students may be encountering. It is designed to help kids get back on track and prepared to excel on SATs. In addition to the personalized online tutoring, it provides teachers access to a curriculum builder portal. This feature not only makes teaching easier but helps accommodate the needs of students requiring more attention or assistance with learning.

It is being utilized in classrooms and considered not only effective in tailoring to individual needs of students but is much more cost effective than hiring tutors. From a budgeting standpoint of school systems, this means that more students can benefit without annual expenses increasing.

Mika

Mika was developed by Carnegie Learning and focuses on college math. It is an AI-based tutoring tool that helps students who are struggling in specific subjects or who need access to more in-depth lessons. The goal of Mika is to coach students until the math is actually learned, moving away from the memorization aspects that do not serve well long-term.

It is easily customized to the needs of individual students and closes the gap for students who would normally benefit from tutoring classes or those who are likely to get left behind in the larger classroom setting. The app works much like Thinkster Math by analyzing the information a student puts in and with that information, algorithms determine the specific areas in which a student is struggling and tailors it to his or her needs.

Mika Founders

Mika was founded by computer scientists of Carnegie Mellon University, Carnegie Learning. These scientists are devoted to improving cognitive skills for students. They base much of their application development on feedback gathered from students and teachers and work tirelessly to understand the different ways in which people learn so the software can accommodate for variations of that.

Technology is everywhere, and it will continue to be a part of our lives. When instructors grasp the advantages of AI freeing their time to focus on the more important parts of learning versus being fearful of or intimidated by it, not only will their lives be improved, but also the lives and futures of the students who depend on them for appropriate education and preparation for the future.

Netex Learning
Netex began in 1997 and operate on an international level helping companies with digital solutions that address educational needs whether for management training in corporations or the restructuring of consulting services. Netex also helps teachers through the making lessons and study materials accessible across multiple devices. In addition to this, they provide interactive virtual training and online instructor assessments.

Screen Time Learning
This is an app that is controlled by parents and provides a way for parents to put limits on screen time for kids. The app is complete with math and science quizzes and requires questions to be answered correctly before children gain access to mobile devices.

Screentime was co-founded by Gene Swank as a way to encourage kids to learn in a fun way while helping parents regain control on the amount of time mobile devices are being used by children as well as placing browsing limitations on the devices.

The basis of this program is to help find a healthy balance of using technology and participating in other activities. This is well justified too, with current statistics indicating that children are plugged in at least seven hours every single day.

Screen Time Features
Screen Time is a great example of how AI can positively influence learning for children while also being a useful supervisory tool for parents.

In addition to limiting screen use and putting safety features in place, Screen Time has other features that inspire children to participate in other activities. These include:

- Food Preparation: Kids can earn bonus time to use their devices by helping in the kitchen.
- Making Phone Calls: Children of all ages currently experience discomfort in talking on the phone. This is largely due to texting, emailing, etc. and it is affecting the way and frequencies of families staying in contact. Younger children sometimes try their best to avoid speaking on the phone with long-distance relatives, but with this app, making a phone call to Grandma can be added to a task list. Upon completion of the task list, bonus time is available, and the child has also made that familial contact that they will one day appreciate when they get older; not to mention how much it meant to Grandma.
- Bedtime Blocker: This feature ensures kids won't use the devices too close to bedtime to allow for ample time in winding down.

With this use of artificial intelligence, Screen Time is the bad guy enforcing the rules instead of it always being mom or dad.

The Mandarin Project
Many of us realize that the best way to learn is by being immersed in the environment. The Rensselaer Polytechnic Institute took this to heart and joined IBM in a program referred to as The Mandarin Project. Students are able to experience the Mandarin culture by becoming completely immersed in the culture through the means of virtual reality. In this virtual world, students must practice speaking the Mandarin language and interacting with AI characters in the program.

In this environment, the instructor is actually the computer rather than an individual, with the reasoning being that students may learn easier and faster because the fear of being judged by a professor or embarrassed by classmates in the event of mistakes is non-existent.

Additionally, the students receive immediate feedback from the virtual instructor by offering correct answers and even coaching on proper pronunciation and word usage, which has proven beneficial in the learning process. This program is still in the early developmental stages, but it has been successful.

Innovative Modes of Using AI in Education

Innovation is a vital part of education and keeps learning exciting and challenging for students of all ages.

The Importance of Preparing Students

The profession of teaching is one that is most commonly pursued from the sheer devotion and dedication to making a difference in the lives of students. With many having personally been inspired by a teacher, they are driven to do the same for someone else, hoping to pay it forward to one or many. Therefore, that devotion and desire should also be willing to embrace the technological advancements that we experience on a daily basis in this lifetime.

In today's world, technology is such an integral part of our lives, completely transforming how we function in both the personal to professional environments. Even though there was a period of time when having computer skills was above and beyond in the business world, it is now commonplace. And for today's younger generations, the necessity for them to be not only familiar with such skills but also well-versed in the utilization of artificial intelligence will be the norm. That is why it is so vital that students of all ages are exposed to it through schooling.

Moving Past the Traditional Electronic Devices

In Singapore, they took the AI teacher's assistant to the next level and introduced robots to the classrooms. These robots are useful in relieving teachers of small, repetitive tasks and they also help children transition to the classroom setting. They are screen-free, which also removes hesitations from parents who are fearful of kids being in front of screens too frequently.

Preschool Exposure

The Chinese government provided Singapore preschools with robots and the "PlayMaker" program that is engineered to help with preparing the children in engineering, math, science, and technology. The preschool robots are preprogrammed to handle small tasks such as shining lights, moving in specific directions and/or reading barcodes on toys and responding according to the instructions encoded in the barcodes.

For example, a small plastic robot that has sensors and lights is referred to by the name Kibo and another small robot is in the shape of a bumblebee is called Bee-Bot. Bee-Bot can identify colors or make simple sounds like "beep." The preschoolers learn to command the robot and also participate in exercises with other children to accomplish specific tasks. These tasks are designed to teach the kids sequencing skills that will be used in math and literacy.

The preschool teachers have to attend training to equip them with information, so the PlayMaker programmed robots can be incorporated into the curriculum.

Additionally, some of the Singapore preschools have been equipped with humanoid robots that are programmed to interact with the children. The robot is never depleted of patience when the same question is asked repeatedly by the children and is also able to read stories to the kids.

Kindergarten Use
In kindergarten classrooms, robots were introduced to take on a variety of tasks. Such tasks include reading stories to the children and posing logic problems to them. The robots have also helped some kids overcome shyness by encouraging them to take part in group activities. Also, the class assistants played an important role in helping autistic children break out of their shells socially.

AI Experiment Using Facial Recognition in Schools
In 2017, China set out on a mission to become the world-leader for implementing AI in education, society and even industry by the year 2030. Some of these newer innovations have been put in the school systems and tested by children.

One such test is that of facial recognition. The program has been deployed in high schools and is designed to monitor students' facial expressions and analyze their level of involvement during class. The system is extremely detailed, being referred to as "the intelligent classroom behavior management system." It is programmed to detect seven different moods ranging from afraid, sad, happy, or angry. The AI program is set up to scan the classroom every few seconds and analyze the expressions of students.

In addition to being capable of determining moods, it can also identify actions such as listening, writing, reading, standing up or leaning over a desk. While there is much controversy that stems from the use of facial recognition across other parts of the world, China is welcoming the opportunity.

According to reports, the vice principal of the school, Zhang Guanchao has stated that the data compiled from the AI system has helped teachers improve their methods of instruction to increase the level of engagement from students. He also said that it has improved attendance records and provides information useful in reprimanded children who are "slacking off."

Students have also acknowledged that they are paying closer attention in class because of the monitoring in place.

AI Helps with Essay Grading
Even though the western world has been somewhat reluctant to trust the computer grading systems past the use of multiple choice, there are more than sixty thousand schools in China that are testing AI machine-learning software on essay grading.

During the past decade this machine-learning software has continuously been refined and according to the South China Morning Post, educators are hard pressed to see the difference between system grading versus that of humans.

The use of automated marking systems is not new, as it has been used for multiple choice grading for more than twenty years. However, it is not capable of grading abstract work including essays. With China actively working towards their goal, they are devoting time towards making improvements on the neural network grading system by adding the essay works of more than a million students into the system. This process is meant to train the system by analyzing the plethora of information it has available, with the hope that it will have the ability to remove small human variations in grading.

Advanced Tracking Ability

Between the facial recognition analysis and the grading systems that China is working so diligently to perfect, the potential of other ways it can be used is indeed frightening. In fact, their goal is for the system to be used as a way of tracking the learning progress among students.

Also, there is speculation that the government would use the data to sync up with China's "social credit system," which determines an individual's ability to use the internet and travel.

The creation of this system has been in the works for quite some time and is said to be put into place by the year 2020. Currently with much of the grading being done by humans and speculation of bias playing a role, if the machine-learning systems can be perfected, that possibility will be removed from the equation.

Emerging Ways that AI is Shaping the Future of Education

Technology has excelled drastically over the past couple of decades, and in many ways it has increased conveniences and sped up an array of processes, affecting us in all aspects of life. And, with the ever-growing urge to make improvements in experiences, and also enhance methods and efficiencies, there is no sign of it stopping.

With this in mind, it is crucial that we resist the tendencies to reject the inevitable and risk missing out on a multitude of opportunities. As far as the realm of education, the use of artificial intelligence is focused on assisting teachers in overcoming current barriers that prevent each and every student from receiving the best education possible.

The Effect of AI in the Classroom

It should not be surprising that there is an ongoing debate of the effects of screen time and challenges in defining the appropriate amount that is safe. With so many differing opinions among parents, teachers, and psychologists it is difficult to predict the speed in which artificial intelligence will become routine in education; again, not as a replacement for teachers but in the form of tools. According to the Artificial Intelligence Market in the US Education Sector, by 2021, the presence of Ai in schools will grow by 47.5%.

Efficiency Will Be Increased

The school system, as a whole, is frequently faced with challenges including teacher burnout, teacher shortages and even the lack of high-quality teachers. In addition to that, are the diverse needs of students, with some requiring more one on one interaction. Overall, teachers choose the profession as a way to help enrich the lives of children, whether in a preschool setting, nurturing toddlers, a grade school setting where individuals feel called to make a positive impact on growing children or in higher education when the calling is geared more towards preparing young adults for enjoying success in the professional world.

Regardless of the age range that teaching effects, if new tools are developed, it makes sense to embrace those new tools in the interest of learning. Many teachers experience burnout due to the mere demand of grading in regard to the teacher/student ratio, so if there are innovations that help improve efficiencies and decrease the level of hands-on requirements, why not take advantage of it? For others, it is an ongoing frustration of seeing the needs of students but lacking the time, energy and resources in which to address those needs; but, with the use of technology, some of those shortcomings can be overcome.

AI Assists Faculty
Regardless of apprehensions by some, artificial intelligence is real and continuously expanding. The design of artificial intelligence is powered by the use of algorithms and while the desire of a teacher is to personally help students; that is not always physically possible, especially in the world of higher education where teacher to student ratio is sometimes extreme.

Introduction to Smart Content Programs
In some ways, artificial intelligence is still in the very early stages of becoming a fundamental part of the daily classroom

Many universities are already taking advantage of the machine learning teaching assistants, which are not only beneficial to the instructors but are enriching the lives of students. How? Erik Anderson, a computer science assistant professor at Cornell University, developed a computer program to assist math instructors in determining the process in which students derived at the wrong answers to math problems. This computer program has been used by instructors at the Universities of Washington and Pennsylvania as well as Microsoft and it equips instructors with more in-depth feedback by assessing the thought process of a student and working backward to see what went wrong in the calculations. Not only does this have the potential to reduce the time spent grading paperwork, but it also pinpoints possible weaknesses in the teaching concepts, so improvements can be made.

Encourages Faculty Involvement

The intended purpose of the AI assistant is to enhance the job of instructors. So, it is sensible to encourage involvement from faculty during the development process. This will directly alleviate apprehensions and fears of being replaced by AI, while also providing opportunities for instructors to gain a better understanding of the intended direction for artificial intelligence in the education system.

The entire premise of AI in the educational environment is to improve the teacher-student experience and also equip the student with more opportunities to reach higher levels of learning.

It is quite unlikely that artificial intelligence will replace teachers in the near future because human interaction is still vital to the education of students. Therefore, the more teachers are willing to open their minds to the variety of ways that AI can enhance the scholastic environment, the better it will be for instructors, students, and our future leaders.

Below are several ways artificial intelligence will shape the future of education.

Personalized Learning

The current education system is designed to group students by age, which ultimately disregards the distinctions concerning those that learn at a different pace or have varying talents or interests. Consequently, the typical classroom setting results in some students struggling to grasp what is being said while others are bored because they comprehended it early on.

Educators have had a long-time desire to adjust methods of teaching that would address the particular needs of individual students, but time and budgeting have often been a constraint. Education should not be viewed as a one-size-fits-all solution and artificial intelligence can actually assist in providing insight into the needs of individual students without necessarily requiring more dedicated time from the instructor.

Smart Content and ITS Programs
Companies including Carnegie Learning and Content Technologies are devoted to developing applications that involve Smart Content programs so students will have access to personalized learning materials and condense study materials into easily digestible segments.

This expansion of the educational system will also begin to utilize ITS, or intelligent tutoring systems. Personalized learning sessions will be developed based on the analysis of student's performance levels. The goal of ITS is primarily aimed towards higher-education and will eventually act as replacement courses, while still offering real-time feedback on the progress of students.

Personalization Bridges the Gap
The use of artificial intelligence can help bridge this gap between teacher and student, designing study material that will help fill the void. AI makes this possible since it can be programmed to provide more personalized and adaptive learning platforms.

During the early education years, the perception that children learn in different ways, varying capacities and in various ways is widely accepted. This is validated when you consider the hands-on learning techniques that are offered in children's museums and specialized school programs that incorporate teachings using the seven learning styles; spatial, auditory, linguistic, kinesthetic, mathematical, interpersonal and intrapersonal. Yet, higher education models let those techniques fall by the wayside and focus on the "one module guide for all" model.

The different models for learning should not be tossed aside as students grow but rather they should be acknowledged and incorporated into the teaching processes. However, in order to achieve this goal, the input and cooperation of teachers are required so AI platforms can be designed accordingly. Additionally, AI cannot teach the concepts of human interaction and communication skills.

Thus, when teachers partake in the development of the computer programs that will accommodate for and address items that do not require hands-on attention, they will have more time available to focus on lecture formats and ways to integrate interaction and presentation aspects. Again, AI is intended to be a useful tool for teachers not a way to replace them.

When you consider how AI affects our lives on a personal level, such as Netflix suggesting shows based on the history of what we have watched, we welcome that and perceive it as a convenience. Basically, Netflix personalized recommendations according to viewing habits, which reduces the amount of time spent searching for something to watch. Most of us view that as a positive experience. So, why not incorporate that technology into the educational system? Imagine personalizing the learning journey of each student based on their needs, interests, etc., while allowing them to move at their own pace?

Assistance with Grading

It is a common complaint within the education system, that grading the work of students is by far the most daunting of all tasks required within the job of teaching. This is not a complaint necessarily, but more so the dread of repetitiveness, and albeit an important part of the job, it takes away from the time and energy that could actually be spent teaching and interacting with students. So, when you look at it from the teacher standpoint, there is one teacher to 20 or more students, grading the same tests, projects or papers for each and every student multiple times. Grading papers can consume a large bulk of time.

Automation Frees Time

In fact, a study conducted in Germany estimated that teachers spent an average of 1000 hours grading work each year. Consider for a moment the 40-hour work week in America tallies to 2080 hours annually, which means almost half of a teacher's time is devoted to compiling grades rather than educating, year after year. That is time that could be better used doing what he or she pursued their teaching career for, which is offering personalized and impactful instruction. Apart from the frustration and dissatisfaction of teachers, oftentimes, students feel that the grades they received were subjective or erratic.

While the concept of using AI to grade standardized testing formats may be acceptable, the question of how it would be incorporated into the grading of essays and other assignments that are not so straightforward is frequently at the forefront. Surprisingly, this too has been addressed through a process known as AES, or automated essay scoring.

This methodology is designed to measure word count and check spelling errors, but the evaluation process is still being formulated. However, in 2012, the William and Flora Hewlett Foundation conducted a competition that involved teachers physically grading essays of students, while the same essays were graded via the AES system; and the results were an 81% consistency between actual teachers and AI software.

Again, AI is not meant to replace teachers, but to be incorporated as useful tools in the educational environment.

24/7 Student Support

Imagine, if teachers had an assistant that would be available to send out information and reminders to students, or answer common questions regarding the course syllabus at all hours, day or night? Or, what about an assistant that posed questions to students that would spark a lively discussion during the next class session? Such an assistant would not only reduce the teacher workload but would also make a positive impact on the experience of the student.

Creation of the First Teacher's Assistant

This is exactly what happened with Jill Watson, a teaching assistant that was developed at Georgia Tech by Professor Ashok Goel along with a team of graduate students in 2015. The inspiration came from Goel's need to address a multitude of student inquiries regarding an online course. The man-hours required to address the forum posts of 300 students was somewhat inundating, so Jill Watson was invented.

Goel and the selected graduate students created the first teacher's assistant by compiling all the messages students had submitted to the forum which totaled to over 40,000. This data gave Ms. Watson vital information that helped her "learn" what the students would likely ask. As with anything, Ms. Watson had to be "groomed" and "taught" over a period of time to ensure she could accommodate the needs of the students; so, the team set out to make the necessary adjustments to her program in a way that would be most beneficial to the students.

Naturally, the development team had to refine her program to ensure she would be a help rather than a hindrance. Initially, every answer that Ms. Watson formulated had to be reviewed by the team prior to it being posted on the forum, but with their dedication and her ability to learn, once she reached 97% accuracy in her answers, they leveled her up with the clearance to post directly to the forums.

Interestingly enough, is that during the initial launch of the Jill Watson program, students were unaware that they were interacting with a computer program. When the students were informed, needless to say, there were an array of responses and at this point, Ms. Watson has received multiple nominations for best teacher's assistant award.

Teachers and Students Benefit
The concept of students having access to an online tutor around the clock also offers peace of mind to parents by resolving the issue of working through those algebra or calculus problems during the midnight hours. Some parents struggle with having the ability to help their kids with homework, but this type of support would fix that.

Having access to teaching assistants in every classroom would not replace teachers but would relieve them of the more mundane tasks that eat into valuable time.

Expanding Learning Spaces
With the progression of educational AI development, the classroom will no longer be constricted to four walls, and instead, learning can take place well beyond the classroom. Eventually, students will have the flexibility to learn wherever and whenever they want. This style of learning will benefit individuals from many walks of life, such as those who lack the financial means of attending college, or due to personal commitments are unable to pursue a college education in the traditional setting.

Many educational institutions are already implementing "smart" classroom spaces that include laptops, whiteboards, multiple projectors and monitors that incorporate an interactive style of learning. This setup, which is equipped with AI platforms gives instructors the advantage of being able to nurture the new methods of learning, providing students with a mixture of face to face instruction along with online interaction.

Customer Service Enhancements
Artificial intelligence also helps streamline many processes that improve customer service. From the teacher's assistant, Jill Watson being available to answer student questions 24/7, to the admissions process being simplified with other AI programs, response time is shortened, and questions are answered immediately; offering an optimal experience for students and parents.

Educational institutions including private schools, primary schools, and colleges are frequently overburdened with immense administrative tasks. Consider the number of students that may attend a single school and then account for the masses of paperwork required for each student from admission paperwork, applications for enrollment and the time-sensitivity involved.

Whereas much of the work is performed by individuals, universities and other institutions have adopted an AI platform similar to what human resource departments use in managing job applications. The system works by filtering through batches that meet certain criteria at which point, hired staff steps in to complete the process.

Just as teachers are immersed in numerous responsibilities, administrative staff are also consumed with taskwork. With the assistance of AI, some of this workload is reduced.

Campuses Take It A Step Further

The AI assistance present on college campuses is not limited to helping teachers and administrative staff. Some are also using it in a way that helps freshmen settle into the new life of attending a college. For example, Arizona State University is using AI-enabled Voice Assistants. Students are equipped with their own Amazon Alexa device that has uses an app specifically designed by the institution to address common questions and also provide information about events and other pertinent campus details.

Can Make Learning Less Intimidating

Oftentimes the best way of learning is by making mistakes and that is true no matter the age. However, in the traditional school setting, learning through trial and error is intimidating for some and in extreme cases, making mistakes in front of a group of peers actually causes students who are extremely shy or have a lack of self-esteem to completely shut down. The mere thought of being put on the spot is paralyzing and even if these students know the correct answers, they aren't able to convey them in a public setting.

However, when AI is used in a way that assists students in the learning process, the non-physical instructor is less likely to be perceived as judgmental while also providing tips for improvement.

Data Mining Works Towards Student Selection

Data mining is already used by companies that focus on retail, communication, marketing, etc. by compiling information about consumer purchases, pricing preferences, and product interests. This process equips businesses with a way to target specific audiences and cater to their interests as a way of increasing sales and customer loyalty.

Now, it is also being used in the educational field as a way of selecting students for specific courses based on individual grades and academic goals. Colleges are embracing this technique of smart-data gathering and using the information to target prospective students as well as help engage existing students.

Additionally, these data mining systems are being used experimentally as a way to provide transitional training to students that will ease them away from the high school classroom environment to the college setting.

Not only will artificial intelligence help students, but educators have access to courses directed towards personal development which can be attended via virtual global conferences. AI may not be as entangled into the educational sector as it is in other areas, but the adoption of it in several areas of the learning culture is well on the way.

Pros and Cons of Using AI in Education

Many of the technological advancements have made a positive impact in our lives, from the added conveniences of voice recognition and the virtual personal and teachers assistants to self-driving cars as well as the reactive machines used in games for our entertainment. Some forms of artificial intelligence indeed make our lives easier.

However, there are some hesitations abound it as well; many of which stem from misunderstandings or unrealistic views developed because of science fiction. The overall hope of the researchers dedicated to expanding the uses of artificial intelligence is motivated by the sheer desire to produce applications that can improve lives, not replace jobs or the people that use the AI applications.

As with anything AI does have both pros and cons associated with it which we will review here.

Pros

#1 Virtual Reality Possibilities: Virtual reality has come a long way in recent years. While researchers dabbled in it as long ago as the 1960s, it was launched to the public in 2012 with the Kickstarter Oculus Rift headset. Since then VR has been incorporated into various fields, not only on the entertainment scale but also in the learning aspects of the medical, health, physical therapy and architectural environments.

The learning possibilities with virtual technology are vast, allowing individuals to visit places and participate in experiences in a 3D virtual world that fills the senses while expanding knowledge.

#2 Time Efficiency: When AI is used to complete repetitive tasks, such as grading assignments, instructors can use that time instead to focus on teaching.

#3 Personalization: AI learning programs can be customized to accommodate the individual personalities of students, based on the pace and style in which they learn best. From the teaching standpoint, the consistent analytical data compiled within these courses provide better insight to the instructor about each student.

#4 Twenty-four Hour Access: Students have access to AI teaching assistants around the clock. This is a major benefit for students with varying schedules, as each one of us has our own personal biorhythm.

#5 Reduction in Errors: Errors are a part of human nature. Regardless of how much care is taken in something, we are not perfect. However, since AI is based solely on algorithms, human error is not a factor.

#6 Individual Student Selection: Specialized classes for students who are more academically driven have existed for decades; being selected through testing, which requires time from instructors. With AI, talented and motivated students can be selected through data assessment that is automatically compiled. For example, suppose an instructor is seeking a few individuals who are particularly driven or possess specific qualities available to perform a difficult task, yet he has six separate classes of students. Rather than evaluating each student from all six classes, the AI technology is able to produce reports for easy selection.

#7 Expanded Outreach: With AI being integrated into the education system and virtual presence devices becoming more readily available, students with physical disabilities, or those unable to attend a standard class setting would be able to participate in the education platform more easily.

#8 Closes the Language Gap: Artificial intelligence provides a way to close the gap of a language barrier with real-time translation. Having this accessible in the classroom would improve interaction among a group and prevent the individuals learning a new language from feeling isolated.

Cons

#1 Experience Does Not Affect Quality: While teachers become better over the course of time, through experience, because AI is based strictly on algorithms, the amount of experience does not affect the quality of output.

#2 Encourages Technology Addiction: Technology addiction has already made a negative impact on social interaction for many and when we encourage more usage with AI devices, this may worsen. Whereas the classroom has typically been a place that bans technology and encourages children to learn in traditional ways, this will be reduced with AI.

#3 Reduces Personal Interaction: As technology replaces some of the tasks of instructors, the interaction between student and teacher will be reduced somewhat, and it is this personal interaction with teachers that so many individuals have credited for positive changes in their lives.

#4 Unemployment: While the intention of AI in the education system would be to improve efficiencies for teachers by replacing repetitive tasks, if staffing is affected than many teachers will become unemployed. Currently, there are more than three million educators in the United States alone, so the potential changes due to these technological advancements may be worrisome.

#5 Lack of Flexible Teaching Methods: From the human standpoint, teachers can approach various instructional methods to help a student understand whereas an AI platform is strictly based on algorithms and therefore would not be equipped to offer flexibility in this way.

#6 Hands-on Skills Are Reduced: As technology continues to make things easier for us, the hands-on skills and experience necessary to function without it will be drastically reduced. If the teaching of basics is forfeited, society as a whole will suffer.

#7 Less Accountability: With the implementation of AI in the classroom, there is the potential for less accountability and perhaps less motivation from the student. Oftentimes, students are driven to complete a project early and put forth their best efforts because they want to impress their teachers. Again, with the reduction in human interaction, will students become less motivated, or will they be more driven at the thought of working at their own pace and not being held back? That is yet to be determined.

There is never a perfect scenario with anything. All in all, if artificial intelligence is developed so that it provides students with more opportunities and assists instructors by alleviating much of the repetitive work, then it is conceivable, the pros will far outweigh the cons.

Embracing the Educational Opportunities of AI

Overall, teachers as a whole chose the path as a way to directly and positively affect students and guide them to a positive future. And, in regard to that future, the fact of the matter is that with most jobs, even entry-level positions, require a minimum of a basic college education. Therefore, it is the responsibility of the educational institutions to implement processes that will reach students in the best ways possible to provide them a sufficient education. Not only is the use of artificial intelligence more affordable than additional staffing, but there is also the prospect of being able to reach a more diverse group of people in effective ways.

AI Helps Overcome Teaching Challenges
As previously addressed, artificial intelligence is already assisting educational instructors with some of the more repetitive aspects of teaching through automation.

School systems everywhere experience challenges from teacher shortages, lack of quality teachers and funding constraints. When the availability of AI technology can enrich the educational system, why not embrace it? AI programs that are able to identify where the learning shortfalls are for students and customize a program that is tailored to individual learning styles actually eliminates the need for a teacher to devote hours of time in physically evaluating and in the end drawing the same conclusion.

Also, consider, in the past, when a teacher had several tests to grade that previously required hours of time, conducting the repetitive process for each paper and now AI can complete the same tasks speedily and accurately without becoming fatigued. Why not utilize it? Taking advantage of such technology provides instructors the freedom to avoid losing personal time with family or failure to make the most of the following teaching day due to lack of sleep the night before grading papers.

AI Fills the Gap When There is a Shortage of Expert Teachers

In order for students to excel, they must have access to high-quality curriculum and skilled educators. Through the use of online resources, even where there is a shortage of highly skilled teachers, the less experienced teachers will still be equipped to provide students with quality education.

High-quality teachers acquired their expertise either through natural talents or over the course of time through practice and even trial and error. Those that have taught for years have also likely developed techniques that help them accommodate for an assortment of individual student needs, but traditional methods still pose limitations.

In a teacher survey conducted, 84% of teachers stated that implementing a variety of techniques into the daily curriculum in order to meet the learning needs of different students was very difficult. Fortunately, with the use of technology, AI assistants, automated assessment and lesson plan software, the needs of students can be more easily met. This technology is helping us revamp the educational system and move away from standardized processes that have frequently failed.

Tech Industry Needs AI-Skilled Graduates

In a report published by LinkedIn in August 2018, it was announced that DataCamp raised $25 million for the purpose of creating courses for data science.

DataCamp is an online platform that offers courses to students in the data science field. Many universities use the DataCamp platform, including Brigham Young University. The online courses are developed by world experts who specialize in the field of data science and machine learning applications.

The shortage of individuals exceeds more than 150,000 people and with large firms such as IBM predicting growth of more than twenty-percent in AI, the heat is on to provide educational opportunities that will equip graduates with the necessary skills to fulfill such positions.

The funding that DataCamp received was provided by Spectrum Equity, a company recognized for producing and scaling successful online courses including Lynda.com and Teachers Pay Teachers. While DataCamp provides online courses to students, they also cater to businesses that support and encourage continuing education among employees.

CEO of the company, Jonathan Conelissen hopes to play a vital role in fulfilling the educational needs that will help grow the global online community. This kind of financial support towards AI education should be an indication of the importance of preparing kids for the array of new skills required for them to have a successful life.

Schools Need to Take Advantage of AI
Experts are beginning to apply the pressure for schools to incorporate AI into lesson plans. A spokesperson for the University of Roehampton and a key player in the development of computing education, Miles Berry expressed his disappointment in the lack of opportunity being presented within the schools.

Berry went on to state that even if access to AI resources may be challenging, it is not difficult to add virtual assistants to classrooms. With the VA devices including Amazon's Alexa, Apple's Siri, or the Google Assistant being affordable and easy to set up, there is no reason why these shouldn't be utilized as a chance to expose children to the more simplified versions of AI.

The entities that provide higher education are now seeing the dire need of offering the various AI learning platforms to students because within a few short years, these students will be working adults. However, it is extremely important in the education of younger generations too.

Bottom line AI needs to become a part of the core curriculum and teachers need to be taught how to best incorporate it into their daily lessons. With the advancement of tech companies and with manufacturing roles being replaced with automation, the approach needs to be updated and remodeled rapidly. Otherwise, the children of today and our future leaders will be the ones who ultimately pay the price.

4 Future-Proof Skills

AI is smart, no doubt about it. Humans are smarter! One key factor to keep in mind, AI is only as smart and capable as the individuals who programmed the rules and parameters which govern the AI itself. There are numerous skills which educators can develop which cannot be replaced by a computer. Continuing your mastery of the four skills outlined in this section may give you an advantage over AI. These future-proof skills reflect on some of the key tenants of human intelligence. Even with the inevitable rapid adoption of AI in education, doubling down on these skills will help you secure your place in the classroom and beyond.

Skill 1 – Critical Thinking

Critical thinking may be the most important skills one can develop. Helping students think beyond the basics, however, may be one of the greatest challenges facing higher education today.

The Collegiate Learning Assessment Plus (CLA+), a standardized exam created to measure critical thinking skills among university students recently produced evidence highlighting a major deficiency. Very few students who completed the assessment demonstrated improvement between their first and last year in college. This trend was apparent even among universities claiming that critical thinking was a core component of the required curriculum.

This challenge presents a considerable problem for educators to acknowledge and correct. Being a major proponent of critical thinking, warrants a second glance at the CLA+ itself to fully understand what the data is showing. After all, we understand that data can be portrayed in many different ways. So, does this assessment truly forecast a skills gap on the rise?

The CLA+ is offered by over 200 public higher education entities. Although these results are not published, in 2017 The Wall Street Journal acquired the results via a request for public records. The results show the details from the test ranging from 2013 to 2016. The assessment shows considerable gaps between universities and colleges; however, the results do not attempt to explain why some schools perform better or worse than others.

An example in the report by The Wall Street Journal followed Plymouth State University, based in New Hampshire. Between freshmen and seniors, Plymouth State demonstrated the most significant increase in critical thinking skills. When this improvement was further examined, students and faculty at Plymouth State reported that courses were structured without implicit activities related to critical thinking. Plymouth State does provide a framework for critical thinking. This framework leads students to develop skills of systematic inquiry and to independently discover information. The noted improvement in critical thinking skills among students at Plymouth State may be a result of integrating critical thinking into every course as opposed to a singular, dedicated course in critical thinking.

This inquiry-based approach includes problem-solving across multiple subject areas. In one course students conducted a mock-trial of the notorious Lizzie Borden criminal justice case. If you are unfamiliar with this case, Borden was accused but later acquitted of murdering her father and stepmother in 1892. The students in this course were asked to examine many different challenging areas of inquiry including, forensic science, history, law, communications, and others. In complex problem-solving challenges like these, students are encouraged to not just focus on the topic alone. Students are engaged in the process of discovery and evaluation when searching for data and eventually organizing that data into relevant information. The structure of the information and style of presentations utilized also support the development of critical thinking skills.

Plymouth State may have achieved improvements in critical thinking, however, similar examples at other universities did not show the same success. Based on the full scope of The Wall Street Journal review of the Collegiate Learning Assessment data, few schools found success by a using the same broad scope application of critical thinking activities within the curriculum. While Plymouth

State is to be applauded, the critical thinking competency benefits of approach appear to be an anomaly.

If the universal application of critical thinking, infused into higher education practice, is not the right approach... what strategy do educators need to employ? Educators face the challenge of helping students examine, scrutinize, and decode information. Utilizing simulations and "real-world" case studies may help in this pursuit. Additionally, empowering students to draw upon their own conclusions and to use scientific and scholarly, proven research practices that take the long road may also help foster critical thinking skills. Issac Asimov was asked to predict what 2019 would look like 35 years ago, he had this to say, "Schools will undoubtedly still exist, but a good schoolteacher can do no better than to inspire curiosity which an interested student can then satisfy at home at the console of his computer outlet." While there is truth in what Asimov predicted, I believe that an educator can do much more than simply inspire others. Through the process of leading a student's development of critical thinking skills, teachers can help students not only achieve their maximum potential but to also become a catalyst for creating positive social change. No computer on earth can yet replace the quality mentorship a dedicated teacher can provide.

In the instant information age, we are riddled with "alternative facts" and pummeled by an over-reliance on a just "Google it" research philosophy, the process of critical thinking may appear to be cumbersome and counter-productive. Mix into the current process of information gathering, nearly ubiquitous social media platforms which perpetuate the risks of confirmation bias and group think and we now have a formula for an information literacy crisis. I personally struggle to recall the last time I relied on my memory more than my mobile.

The hope and expectation of a college education must be set above and beyond gathering the information one can find on YouTube, Google and other "instant-learning" platforms. It is the hope that graduating students emerge with critical thinking skills, a greater knowledge of ethics, the ability to work as part of a team, and with a spark of leadership experience. Therefore, providing a challenging and intensive educational experience rich with critical thinking must be the key function of higher education.

When we tap into our critical thinking skill-set, we examine all the data and information we are able to gather. In that pursuit of understanding, we often discover that the views we may have previously believed to be true may need to be examined with a different, or a new lens. When I reflect on my personal experiences as a college student, some of the most powerful, lasting memories I have are those moments when my ideas were challenged, and a new-found point of view emerged. If a college education does not change a student's outlook, present a new discovery, or inspire a student to become more than the person they were when they enrolled, why bother? This question consistently re-enforces for me that critical thinking may truly be one of the most important skills a person can develop.

Skill 2 - Design Thinking
One thing that is particularly important to understand about artificial intelligence is that AI lacks empathy. In this regard, AI is not capable of finding all possible solutions to a problem. At the same time, empathy led problem-solving is of major importance in today's world. Therefore, the best solutions are formed by a mastery of design thinking.

Since AI is incapable of relating to or empathizing with human emotions and the human experience, design thinking is necessary in order to enable empathy led problem-solving. Design thinking is an approach that centers around humans and compliments the AI process. By thinking about how human experiences (i.e., people's interpretation) map to data (i.e., AI's interpretation), we're able to establish a deep learning solution that's based on the features of data.

Design Thinking is a massively popular concept thanks to Standford's d.school, IDEO, and others who have promoted it in recent years. Basically, it takes the vast potential that lies within human creativity and it puts it into a highly functional and structured methodology. It encourages a team to be innovative and share ideas with low-risk and rapid iterations that quickly make it to the market.

When it comes to education, there are a few key aspects that should encourage the teaching of design thinking. First and foremost, teaching design thinking preps students for growing complexity that lies in the future of our world. AI is already shaping our world, and learning how to interact with it, and grow with it, is essential.

Generally, it is agreed that there are five stages in Design Thinking. Below, is a summary of each stage.

Stage One - Empathize
The first step in the Design Thinking process is to empathize. This is the key step that lets us discover the opportunities in AI that drive specific and measurable progress to support an end goal. By definition, empathy is a deliberate effort on our part to understand the thoughts and desires of a person or group of people. This includes how they live, how they work, and how they thrive.

Obviously, when it comes to the world of business, there is incredible value in being empathetic. Understanding and examining basic needs and motivations enables a business to then scale products and solutions to match. Observing, engaging, and listening will all be required during this state. Qualitative research will play a big role.

Stage Two - Define
The next step is about analyzing and synthesizing all the information gathered in the previous stage in order to define a core problem. This is the core problem that the next steps will work to address. Cross-functional and human-focused questions will be key to completing this step successfully. A design thinker will aim to reach a point-of-view statement or a problem statement. This is a

statement that defines the problem and also frames it in a way to invite creative solutions for it.

This is where an AI project has to show the data behind the problem. This step starts with the data an organization currently has. The toughest part is getting clean data, but once the data has been cleaned, its features can be extracted. This step can then be completed as the process moves on to the Ideate stage.

Stage Three - Ideate

After empathizing with the target group and understanding their needs, then identifying a human-centric problem, the third phase can begin. This step is a brainstorming phase where innovative and disruptive solutions need to be uncovered. This phase is less about quality and more about quantity. The more ideas a team is able to generate, the better off they will be.

The goal is not to create a perfect solution. Rather, the goal is to address the problem from multiple angles. Thinking up as many cross-functional solutions as possible is key. Starting with "What if..." questions is a great way to get things moving.

Stage Four - Prototype

After generating a number of ideas, the next step is establishing a systematic way to test and improve the individual aspects of the AI solutions. This typically involves users. Prototyping is a quick and low-cost way to test something and see if it will be adopted by the target audience. Good examples include flowcharts, reports, paper prototypes, UX mockups, visual reports, and so on.

Inexpensive and scaled down versions are key to successful prototyping. This allows the testing and presentation of many different ideas. Oftentimes, not just one idea will pass through the prototyping stage. Rather, the initial ideas will be revamped and even combined based on feedback and further review. These new iterations will likely re-enter into the prototyping process until a final iteration is selected to move on to the next step.

User feedback is definitely essential for successful and worthwhile prototyping. Without it, the prototype selection process would really just be a guessing game.

Stage Five - Test

Finally, design thinking concludes with the testing period. After targeting and approving AI solutions during the prototyping phase, the next step is scaling things up so that the prototype can be turned into a ready-to-launch iteration. Most initial launches will have only some basic features. With time and adoption, new features will be added based on what the users need.

Skill 3 – Improvisation

Creativity, imagination, and expression cannot be replicated by a computer. The thing that makes art great is the creativity behind it. The skill of being creative in your classroom encourages students to think outside of the box. Therefore, creativity is a major skill. It has been said time and time again that every human has the potential to be creative, it's just many learn to block this potential through the lessons and experiences they are taught over time.

For instance, if a child grew up in a very structured household where creativity and "outside thinking" was discouraged, they would be much more likely to block out their creative thinking skills than a child who grew up in a colorful and artsy household where they were encouraged to use their imagination.

Creative thinking is something children will already practice on their own when playing make-believe games and being around other kids. Of course, most kids grow out of this, so in order to keep allowing them to hone their creative thinking skills, kids have to be given the opportunity to begin utilizing their creative thinking skills in other ways.

Creative thinking should continue far beyond a person's childhood because it plays a vital role in being a good problem solver as an adult. If an adult hones their creative thinking skills, they'll also have an easier time thinking up new solutions to complex issues in addition to creating more intuitive designs. In fact, creative thinking bleeds into many aspects of being a good leader and a good worker.

So, how does this play into AI? Artificial Intelligence is branching out into many new realms that were previously untouched by technology. Art is no exception, and it's currently shaking up the playing field. One of the most controversial moves as of yet is when the famous auction house Christie's chose to sell a piece of computer-generated art.

Gideon Kimbrell first wrote about the incident for Forbes and stated, "While many artists were upset with the move, there is little cause for alarm: Like many other applications of the technology, the best use cases will have AI augmenting the efforts of human artists instead of replacing them outright."

The Photoshop software created by Adobe is a good starting point to paint the picture of what augmentation could mean as AI begins further exploring creative fields like artistry. When Photoshop was first launched, many photographers were taken aback by it. Many refused to use it all together. That's because all of them realized it was a huge change in the way things were done.

Many argued that Photoshop meant inauthenticity. They reasoned that, with Photoshop, a photographer could forget about skilled composition and proper exposure, opting to fix those things in the post-processing step instead. Today, you'd be hard pressed to find a photographer that doesn't use Photoshop or another kind of post-processing software to tweak their photos before releasing them.

But, Photoshop doesn't involve AI (yet). The field of AI art is still in its infancy but there is limitless potential. It could very well turn into an art movement that utilizes technological collaboration, marrying the work of both human and machine. This is what should excite artists.

Its unlikely art generated solely by AI will ever catch on for all of the reasons discussed previously--it lacks empathy, it lacks human connection, and it lacks an understanding of the human experience. Instead, AI in art will likely take off through software that brings humans and AI together to make even better pieces that capture new levels of interest.

One proposed AI solution in the world of art does involve photo editing. Prisma is an app that uses neural networks and the power of Artificial Intelligence to transform images and make them look like they were painted on canvas. Rather than just overlaying layers as older software did, Prisma achieves a very realistic effect by actually repainting the pictures.

Vincent is another AI program that analyzes thousands of artworks to understand color, contrast, and brushstrokes. With this knowledge, it can take the work of a human artist and complete it in the style of a famous painter like Vincent van Gogh. Such collaboration is able to not only inspire humans further but also teach them how to yield better pieces of art.

Finally, AI can boost productivity and inspire creativity by utilizing its ability to take over the repetitive tasks that take humans an excessive amount of time to complete. By removing redundancy from processes, humans will have more time and willpower to seek inspiration and be creative. In the world of art, AI could find its place creating templates, backgrounds, or even common visual themes. Thus, saving artists time and giving them the chance to work more ambitiously on new pieces.

Skill 4 – Adaptation
Adaption is the key to survival. For educators, adaption is what helps them continuously learn and improve in their work. After all, with each passing year, the student base changes as does the workforce that they will be entering into and even the materials that they must learn to do so successfully.

Adaption is considered a metacognitive skill. Educators are known for being very adaptive, being able to morph into their surroundings and is widely celebrated for consistently investing and expanding their knowledge. With all of that said, AI stands to help educators embrace and posses a "T-shaped" skill set so that they can enjoy even further success.

When it comes to describing a professional, their skill set is generally said to be either an "I" or a "T". The latter is much more desirable. This is because a "T shaped" skill set means that the person is able to apply a depth of experience and knowledge (represented by the vertical line of the T) to a number of different specialties (represented by the horizontal line of the T). An "I shaped" skill set, on the other hand, lacks cross-disciplinary capabilities and the person likely only specializes in one or two things.

Steve Jobs, the late CEO of Apple, was one of the first to bring the I and T shaped skillsets to light. He pictured people with an I shaped skill set as "narrow and tight", highly specialized in one area. On the other hand, a T shaped skillset is broad and expanded. A person with a T-shaped skill set will demonstrate broader skills and broader knowledge. They will learn by linking up different specialties and perspectives.

For educators, cross-discipline is one of the cornerstones to success. Just off the top of one's head, you could likely list a dozen skills and disciplines that an educator needs to embody in order to be successful in their job. Communication is, by all means, crucial, but so is the ability to explain concepts in various different ways so that they resonate with the different learning styles of students.

A mixture of both skillsets can be found in the average workplace today, but for educators and leaders, having a T-shaped skill set is thought to be very important. This is a perspective that is shared by not only the educators of today but also many HR professionals and famous CEOs.

Andy Boynton wrote for Forbes, "T people are better at fostering the diverse connections and conversations that bring exceptional ideas to the surface. And these leaders bemoan what they see as a dearth of them in today's hyper-specialized environments."

There are plenty of Is in the workforce. The workforce is now calling for more Ts to step up in every single field. That's because a person with a T-shaped skill set is going to be able to better adapt to the constant change that is now being presented with today's technology-driven world.

A person with a T-shaped skill set will be able to better utilize the various tools at their disposal while more quickly being able to solve complex issues and even adapt to using brand new tools and technology as it is released to them. These skills are gradually becoming daily necessities as AI and other systems take up a bigger and bigger part of our interactions.

T-shaped skillsets will help workers interact with and take advantage of such systems thanks to their ability to pull from prior knowledge and similar experiences to meet an end goal.

This isn't to say that a professional should feel it's not worth becoming specialized in any one area. Usually, even a person with a T-shaped skill set will find themselves specialized in one main area of their career. However, they have also spent the time to build out the horizontal bar of the skills diagram, enabling them to be a T person where it counts. This gives a person the "best of both worlds" when it comes to finding opportunities and excelling in their work.

What's Next?

Computers have largely been a part of our lives for the past four decades and during that time, the advances in machine learning have quietly integrated artificial intelligence into our lives. AI has made an entry into education, both in theory and in practice. Market analysis indicates that AI will grow by nearly 60% from 2018 to 2021 and as that growth occurs, new opportunities are emerging to improve and advance educational practices.

When the use of AI is not accepted into our educational system, ultimately it will be students who pay the price. An absence of student career readiness and instructional personalization are already degrading the quality of education today. Overall, AIs main benefit is found in the time-saving nature of the technology in action. Through careful utilization of AI, low value, time-intensive tasks can be automated. This grants teachers and support staff a new advantage that may help them re-focus their energy on personalizing education and improving the total student experience. There is a logical fear that AI will strip us of meaningful human interactions. Relationships are crucial to human development and teachers play a major role in that growth process. AI won't steal our personal relationships, in fact, AI may offer a means to improve them.

While Amazon may have 20% of their work done by robots, the school system will not be affected in the same way. By embracing the benefits of AI technology and focusing on the 4 future-proof skills, what's next for education is exciting and promising. With the implementation of machine learning into education, both teachers and students will benefit.

References

A Medium Corporation (2018, March 12). *10 Pros and Cons of AI in Education*. Retrieved from https://medium.com/@oleksii_kh/10-pros-and-cons-of-ai-in-education-c7c1b69a89b2

Belkin, D. (2017). Exclusive test data: many colleges fail to improve critical-thinking skills. Retrieved from https://www.wsj.com/articles/exclusive-test-data-many-colleges-fail-to-improve-critical-thinking-skills-1496686662

Boynton, A. (2011). *Are you an "I" or a "T"?* Retrieved from https://www.forbes.com/sites/andyboynton/2011/10/18/are-you-an-i-or-a-t/#5f3a78336e88

Brainly. Retrieved from https://blog.brainly.co/

Built In (2018, December 3). *Artificial Intelligence in Education.* Retrieved from https://builtin.com/artificial-intelligence/ai-in-education

Cambridge Consultants. (2018). *Vincent, a deep learning demonstration, building on human input to create completed works of art.* Retrieved from https://www.cambridgeconsultants.com/vincent

Council for Aid to Education. (2019). *Collegiate Learning Assessment Plus.* Retrieved from https://cae.org/flagship-assessments-cla-cwra/cla/

Christensen Institute (2016, December). *Teaching in the Machine Age.* Retrieved from https://www.christenseninstitute.org/wp-content/uploads/2017/03/Teaching-in-the-machine-age.pdf

CTI. Retrieved from http://contenttechnologiesinc.com/

Disruptor Daily (2018, March 5). *How AI is Disrupting Education.* Retrieved from https://www.disruptordaily.com/ai-disrupting-education/

Forbes (2018, July 25). *How Is AI Used in Education?* Retrieved from https://www.forbes.com/sites/bernardmarr/2018/07/25/how-is-ai-used-in-education-real-world-examples-of-today-and-a-peek-into-the-future/#c010a27586e8

IDEO. (2019). *Design Thinking.* Retrieved from https://www.ideou.com/pages/design-thinking

Inside Higher Ed (2018, September 26). *Pushing the Boundaries of Learning With AI.* Retrieved from https://www.insidehighered.com/digital-learning/article/2018/09/26/academics-push-expand-use-ai-higher-ed-teaching-and-learning

ISTE (2018, May 17). *Preparing students for an AI-driven world.* Retrieved from https://www.iste.org/explore/articleDetail?articleid=2197

Ivy.AI (2019). *About.* Retrieved from https://medium.com/@IvyAI/why-i-started-a-chatbot-company-5c3e66d15314

Kimbrell, G. (2017). How drawing became the gateway to AI communication. Retrieved from https://www.forbes.com/sites/forbestechcouncil/2017/11/01/how-drawing-became-the-gateway-to-ai-communication/#46e844842e85

New Atlas (2018, May 27). *AI in Schools: China's Massive Education Experiment.* Retrieved from https://newatlas.com/china-ai-education-schools-facial-recognition/54786/

Prisma. (2019). *About.* Retrieved from https://prisma-ai.com/about.html

Stanford University. (2019) *d-school.* Retrieved from
https://dschool.stanford.edu/

The Tech Advocate (2017, August 22). *5 Examples of Artificial Intelligence in The Classroom.* Retrieved from https://www.thetechedvocate.org/5-examples-artificial-intelligence-classroom/

Tech Target (2018, August). *AI for Education Brings Benefits to Burdened School Staff.* Retrieved from https://searchenterpriseai.techtarget.com/feature/AI-for-education-brings-benefits-to-burdened-school-staff

World Economic Forum (2018, June 18). Teaching AI in Schools Could Equip Children for the Future. Retrieved from https://www.weforum.org/agenda/2018/06/teaching-ai-in-schools-could-equip-students-for-the-future

Made in the USA
Columbia, SC
22 March 2021